Copyright © 2023 by Kelli Tempest (Author)

This book is protected by copyright law and is intended solely for personal use. Reproduction, distribution, or any other form of use requires the written permission of the author. The information presented in this book is for educational and entertainment purposes only, and while every effort has been made to ensure its accuracy and completeness, no guarantees are made. The author is not providing legal, financial, medical, or professional advice, and readers should consult with a licensed professional before implementing any of the techniques discussed in this book. The content in this book has been sourced from various reliable sources, but readers should exercise their own judgment when using this information. The author is not responsible for any losses, direct or indirect, that may occur from the use of this book, including but not limited to errors, omissions, or inaccuracies.

We hope this book has been informative and helpful on your journey to understanding and celebrating older adults. Thank you for your interest and support!

Title: Learning and Academia-The Capitals'
Educational Landscape
Subtitle: Tertiary Education in Each Capital:
Universities and Colleges

Series: Cosmopolitan Chronicles: Tales of the World's
Great Cities
By Kelli Tempest

"The world is a book, and those who do not travel read only one page."
Saint Augustine

"A city is not gauged by its length and width, but by the broadness of its vision and the height of its dreams."
Herb Caen

"The purpose of life is to live it, to taste experience to the utmost, to reach out eagerly and without fear for newer and richer experience."
Eleanor Roosevelt

"The only way to do great work is to love what you do."
Steve Jobs

"Travel makes one modest. You see what a tiny place you occupy in the world."
Gustave Flaubert

"Cities were always like people, showing their varying personalities to the traveler. Depending on the city and on the traveler, there might begin a mutual love, or dislike, friendship, or enmity."
Roman Payne

"The best way to predict the future is to create it."
Abraham Lincoln

"The world is a beautiful book, but of little use to him who cannot read it."
Carlo Goldon

"In every walk with nature, one receives far more than he seeks."
John Muir

Table of Contents

Introduction

Importance of education and academia in the development of a city

Education and academia play a crucial role in the development of any city. They are fundamental components of a city's infrastructure and have a significant impact on its economic, social, and cultural growth. Education is not only essential for personal growth and development, but it also contributes to the progress and prosperity of a society as a whole.

In today's knowledge-based economy, education is more important than ever. It is the key to creating a skilled workforce and a competitive advantage for cities. Education and academia create the conditions for innovation, research, and development, which are crucial for the success of any modern economy. They provide the skills, knowledge, and expertise necessary for people to succeed in a rapidly changing world.

Cities that invest in education and academia tend to have higher levels of economic growth, social cohesion, and cultural diversity. Education helps to reduce poverty and inequality, and it provides individuals with the tools they need to succeed in life. It also helps to create a sense of community and belonging, which is essential for a healthy and prosperous society.

Moreover, education and academia play a critical role in attracting talent and investment to cities. Cities that have a strong education system tend to attract more highly skilled workers and businesses, which in turn creates more job opportunities and contributes to the growth of the local economy. Education and academia also help to create a vibrant cultural and intellectual scene, which is attractive to both residents and visitors.

In addition to economic benefits, education and academia also have a significant impact on social development. Education provides individuals with the knowledge and skills they need to participate fully in society and to make informed decisions. It helps to create a more informed and engaged citizenry, which is essential for a healthy and vibrant democracy.

Education and academia also promote cultural diversity and tolerance. They provide opportunities for people from different backgrounds to come together, share ideas, and learn from one another. This helps to break down barriers and promotes understanding and respect between different communities.

In summary, education and academia are essential components of a city's infrastructure. They provide the skills, knowledge, and expertise necessary for individuals to succeed in a rapidly changing world. They contribute to economic growth, social development, and cultural diversity. Cities that invest in education and academia tend to be more prosperous, innovative, and inclusive. As such, education and academia should be a top priority for any city looking to create a better future for its residents.

Brief overview of the educational landscape of capital cities

Learning and Academia - The Capitals' Educational Landscape is a book that investigates the educational institutions and opportunities available in each capital city, from primary schools to universities. This chapter aims to provide a brief overview of the educational landscape of capital cities, including the types of schools and universities available, the curriculum and teaching methodologies, and the challenges and opportunities in each sector.

Types of Educational Institutions:

The educational landscape of capital cities is diverse, with a range of educational institutions offering different types of education and training. These institutions include public and private primary and secondary schools, universities, vocational and technical schools, and language schools.

Primary and Secondary Schools: Primary and secondary schools in capital cities follow national or state-mandated curricula and are responsible for providing a solid foundation of basic education to their students. In some cities, private schools are also popular, and they often offer a more specialized curriculum or alternative teaching methodologies. Many primary and secondary schools in capital cities also offer extracurricular activities such as sports, music, and drama.

Higher Education Institutions: Capital cities are also home to a range of higher education institutions, including universities, colleges, and research institutions. These institutions offer a variety of undergraduate and graduate degree programs, as well as research opportunities and professional development courses. In many capital cities, the higher education sector is a major contributor to the local economy, attracting students and researchers from around the world.

Vocational and Technical Schools: Vocational and technical schools in capital cities provide specialized training in fields such as healthcare, business, engineering, and technology. These schools offer a range of certificate and diploma programs, as well as apprenticeships and on-the-job training. Vocational and technical schools are essential for providing the skilled workforce needed to support the local economy.

Language Schools: Language schools in capital cities provide instruction in a variety of languages, including English, French, Spanish, and Chinese. These schools offer a range of courses, from basic language instruction to advanced business language courses.

Challenges and Opportunities:

Despite the diversity of educational institutions in capital cities, there are still many challenges that need to be addressed. These challenges include inadequate funding, lack of access to education for marginalized groups, and an overemphasis on standardized testing. However, there are also many opportunities for growth and improvement in the educational landscape, including the use of technology to enhance learning, the development of new teaching methodologies, and greater collaboration between institutions.

Conclusion:

In conclusion, the educational landscape of capital cities is diverse and complex, with a range of institutions offering different types of education and training. While there are challenges to be addressed, there are also many opportunities for growth and improvement. As such, it is important to continue to invest in education and academia to ensure that capital cities remain at the forefront of innovation, development, and prosperity.

Purpose and structure of the book

The purpose of this book is to provide readers with a comprehensive guide to the educational landscape of capital cities around the world. From primary schools to universities, this book will explore the educational institutions and opportunities available in each city, as well as the research and academic culture of each location.

The book is structured into seven chapters, each of which focuses on a specific aspect of education and academia in capital cities. Chapter 1 provides an overview of primary education systems in capital cities, including the curriculum, teaching methodologies, challenges, opportunities, and success stories of primary schools in the cities. Chapter 2 does the same for secondary education, while Chapter 3 provides an overview of higher education systems, including types of institutions, popular courses and programs, challenges, opportunities, and success stories of universities and colleges in the cities.

Chapter 4 focuses on research and innovation culture, highlighting major research institutions and centers, research funding and collaborations, and technological innovation and startups in the cities. Chapter 5 explores study abroad opportunities in capital cities, including popular destinations for international students, scholarships and financial aid for studying abroad, and cultural experiences and benefits of studying in the cities.

Chapter 6 discusses vocational and technical education, including an overview of the system in capital cities, types of programs, job prospects and career opportunities, and challenges and opportunities in vocational and technical education. Chapter 7 explores education policies and governance, including an overview of education policies and governance in capital cities, roles and responsibilities of government and non-governmental organizations, funding and budget allocation for education, and evaluation and improvement of educational programs and policies.

By exploring these different aspects of education and academia in capital cities, this book aims to provide readers with a comprehensive understanding of the educational landscape of different cities around the world, as well as insights into the challenges and opportunities facing education and academia in each location. Whether you are a student, teacher, researcher, policymaker, or simply someone interested in education and academia, this book will provide you with valuable insights into the education systems of some of the world's most influential cities.

Chapter 1: Primary Education

Overview of primary education system in capital cities

Primary education is the first stage of formal education, typically for children between the ages of five and eleven. It lays the foundation for further education and is critical in shaping a child's cognitive, social, and emotional development. In this chapter, we will provide an overview of primary education systems in capital cities around the world.

Capital cities serve as the cultural, economic, and political centers of their respective countries, and as such, they often have unique features and challenges when it comes to primary education. Some cities have large populations, while others have a smaller student population but may face language or cultural barriers. Let's take a closer look at some of the primary education systems in capital cities around the world.

Tokyo, Japan

Japan has one of the highest performing primary education systems in the world, and Tokyo is the capital city that exemplifies this system. The primary education system in Tokyo is known for its rigorous academic standards, which prioritize the teaching of core subjects such as Japanese language, mathematics, science, and social studies. The curriculum is designed to foster a sense of respect for traditional Japanese culture and values.

Primary schools in Tokyo are typically divided into two categories: public schools and private schools. Public schools are free and open to all students, while private schools charge tuition fees and have more selective admission criteria. In general, primary schools in Tokyo have a strong emphasis on developing students' literacy and numeracy skills and fostering a sense of discipline and respect for authority.

London, United Kingdom

The primary education system in London is part of the larger education system in the United Kingdom (UK). Primary schools in London follow the National Curriculum, which covers a wide range of subjects, including English, mathematics, science, history, geography, art, and physical education. Schools in London also place a strong emphasis on the development of social and emotional skills, such as communication, teamwork, and problem-solving.

Primary schools in London are typically divided into two categories: state schools and independent schools. State schools are funded by the government and are open to all students, while independent schools charge tuition fees and have more selective admission criteria. Primary schools in London are known for their diverse student populations, with students from a wide range of cultural, linguistic, and socioeconomic backgrounds.

Beijing, China

China has one of the largest primary education systems in the world, and Beijing is the capital city that exemplifies this system. The primary education system in Beijing is known for its emphasis on academic excellence and discipline. Students are expected to excel in core subjects such as Chinese language, mathematics, science, and social studies.

Primary schools in Beijing are typically divided into two categories: public schools and private schools. Public schools are free and open to all students, while private schools charge tuition fees and have more selective admission criteria. The curriculum in primary schools in Beijing is highly structured and exam-oriented, with a focus on preparing students for the highly competitive secondary education system.

Paris, France

The primary education system in Paris is part of the larger education system in France. Primary schools in Paris follow a comprehensive curriculum that covers a wide range of subjects, including French language, mathematics, science, history, geography, art, and physical education. The curriculum is designed to develop students' critical thinking and problem-solving skills, as well as their cultural and artistic appreciation.

Primary schools in Paris are typically divided into two categories: public schools and private schools. Public schools are free and open to all students, while private schools charge tuition fees and have more selective admission criteria. Primary schools in Paris are known for their small class sizes and emphasis on individualized attention, allowing teachers to tailor their teaching to each student's needs.

Conclusion

Primary education is critical in shaping a child's cognitive, social, and emotional development, and it lays the foundation for their future academic success. While the primary education systems in capital cities vary widely in terms of curriculum, teaching methodologies, and resources, there is a common goal of providing quality education to all children. It is crucial for governments and educational institutions to work together to ensure that primary education is accessible, affordable, and of high quality. By investing in primary education, capital cities can empower their future generations to become responsible and productive citizens who can contribute to the growth and development of their communities.

In conclusion, the primary education systems in capital cities play a critical role in the educational landscape of these cities. This chapter has provided an overview of the primary education system in capital cities, including the curriculum, teaching methodologies, challenges and opportunities, and success stories. It is clear that there are significant differences among the primary education systems in capital cities, and it is essential to continue to research and improve these systems to ensure that all children have access to quality education. The next chapter will focus on the secondary education system in capital cities, providing an overview of its curriculum, teaching methodologies, challenges and opportunities, and success stories.

Curriculum and teaching methodologies

Curriculum and teaching methodologies are essential components of primary education, as they define what students learn and how they learn it. In capital cities, the primary education curriculum varies depending on the country and the specific school system. However, there are some common themes and approaches that can be found across different systems.

One of the key features of primary education curricula in capital cities is a focus on developing foundational skills in literacy and numeracy. These skills are critical for future academic success and are often prioritized in the early years of primary education. In addition to these foundational skills, primary education curricula typically include a range of subjects such as science, social studies, art, and physical education. These subjects are designed to provide a broad and well-rounded education that prepares students for secondary education and beyond.

Teaching methodologies in primary education also vary across capital cities. However, there are some common approaches that are used across different systems. One such approach is active learning, which emphasizes student participation and engagement in the learning process. Active learning methods can include group work, hands-on activities, and project-based learning, which encourage students to take an active role in their own learning.

Another teaching methodology that is commonly used in primary education is differentiated instruction. This approach recognizes that students have different learning styles, interests, and abilities, and that teaching should be tailored to meet the individual needs of each student. Differentiated instruction can involve using a variety of teaching strategies, such as visual aids, manipulatives, and technology, to engage students and help them learn in ways that work best for them.

In some capital cities, there is a growing emphasis on integrating technology into primary education. This can include the use of educational apps, digital textbooks, and interactive whiteboards. Technology can enhance learning by providing access to a wider range of resources, enabling personalized learning experiences, and facilitating communication and collaboration among students and teachers.

In conclusion, primary education curricula and teaching methodologies are crucial components of the educational landscape of capital cities. The curriculum typically focuses on developing foundational skills in literacy and numeracy while providing a broad and well-rounded education. Teaching methodologies aim to engage students and meet their individual needs through active learning and differentiated instruction. With the integration of technology, primary education in capital cities can become more innovative and dynamic, preparing students for success in the 21st century.

Challenges and opportunities in primary education

Primary education is the foundation of a child's learning journey, and ensuring that children receive quality education is essential. However, primary education faces several challenges in capital cities worldwide. These challenges are often interrelated and complex, and addressing them requires significant efforts from the government, educational institutions, teachers, parents, and the wider community.

One of the primary challenges in primary education is the lack of resources, including inadequate funding, outdated or insufficient teaching materials, and limited access to technology. The lack of resources can lead to overcrowded classrooms, where teachers struggle to provide individual attention to each student, resulting in lower academic achievement.

Another significant challenge is the quality of teachers. Primary school teachers play a crucial role in shaping the minds of young learners, but many teachers lack adequate training, skills, and qualifications to effectively teach and manage diverse classrooms. In some cases, the teaching profession is undervalued and underpaid, leading to a lack of motivation among teachers and high turnover rates.

In addition to these challenges, primary education also faces issues related to equity and inclusion. Access to quality education is not always equitable, and marginalized groups, such as children from low-income families, refugees, and minorities, often face barriers in accessing education. Moreover, the lack of inclusivity in teaching practices can lead to discrimination and exclusion, which can affect the learning outcomes of these children.

Despite these challenges, primary education in capital cities also presents several opportunities for improvement. Many educational institutions and organizations are implementing innovative teaching methods and technologies to enhance the learning experience of children. Collaborative learning, gamification, and the use of digital tools are some of the approaches being used to make learning more engaging and effective.

Furthermore, efforts to improve teacher training and qualifications can also lead to better learning outcomes for children. Investing in the professional development of teachers, providing incentives and recognition, and creating a supportive work environment can lead to a more motivated and effective teaching workforce.

Overall, primary education in capital cities faces several challenges, but there are also opportunities for improvement. By addressing the challenges and capitalizing on the opportunities, primary education can provide children with the foundation they need to succeed in their academic and personal lives.

Success stories of primary schools in the cities

There are numerous examples of successful primary schools in capital cities worldwide that have implemented innovative approaches and strategies to enhance the quality of education and provide students with the best possible learning experiences. In this section, we will explore some of these success stories, highlighting their key features and the impact they have had on the students, teachers, and the broader community.

One such success story is the Lycée Français de Singapour, a French international school in Singapore that provides primary education to students aged three to eleven. The school has an excellent reputation for its bilingual program, which offers instruction in both French and English. The curriculum is designed to develop critical thinking and problem-solving skills, and the school has a strong focus on STEM education, with state-of-the-art facilities and resources to support this. The school also places a strong emphasis on extra-curricular activities, including sports, music, and drama, which help to develop well-rounded students.

Another successful primary school is the Copenhagen International School in Denmark, which offers primary education to students from over 80 nationalities. The school has a student-centered approach, with a focus on personalized learning, project-based activities, and interdisciplinary learning. The curriculum is designed to be challenging and engaging, with a strong emphasis on the development of creativity, critical thinking, and social skills. The school has a well-equipped library, an outdoor learning area, and a range of specialist facilities, including a music room, an art room, and a science laboratory.

The West Island School in Hong Kong is another successful primary school that has implemented innovative strategies to enhance the quality of education. The school offers a bilingual program in English and Chinese, with a strong focus on the development of language skills. The curriculum is designed to be inquiry-based, with a focus on project-based learning, problem-solving, and critical thinking. The school has a well-established community service program, which encourages students to get involved in social and environmental initiatives.

These success stories demonstrate that primary education can be enhanced through innovative approaches that focus on the development of key skills and provide students with a well-rounded education. By adopting best practices and sharing success stories, primary schools in capital cities worldwide can learn from each other and work towards providing the best possible education for their students.

Chapter 2: Secondary Education
Overview of secondary education system in capital cities

Secondary education is the next stage of schooling after primary education, typically catering to students between the ages of 12 and 18. In capital cities around the world, the secondary education system is usually more structured and rigorous than the primary system. This is because secondary education is often seen as a preparatory stage for higher education or the workforce, where students are expected to develop a more specialized skill set and gain a deeper understanding of academic subjects.

The secondary education system in each capital city can vary depending on factors such as cultural and economic background, government policies, and historical development. In some cities, the secondary education system may be dominated by public schools, while in others, private schools may play a more significant role. Additionally, some cities may offer specialized programs, such as vocational or technical education, within the secondary education system.

Despite these differences, most secondary education systems share some common characteristics. The curriculum in secondary schools typically covers core subjects such as mathematics, science, social studies, and language arts, as well as electives in areas like the arts, foreign languages, or physical education. Teaching methodologies also vary, but many schools use a combination of lectures, group discussions, and hands-on projects to engage students and encourage critical thinking.

Overall, secondary education plays a crucial role in preparing students for their future careers and higher education. A strong secondary education system can provide students with a solid foundation of knowledge and skills, as well as the ability to think critically and solve problems. As such, it is important to understand the secondary education system in each capital city to better appreciate the opportunities and challenges that students face as they continue their education journey.

Curriculum and teaching methodologies

Secondary education builds on the foundation of primary education and is a crucial phase of a student's academic journey. In capital cities, secondary education typically lasts for four to five years, and students are between the ages of 12-18. The curriculum and teaching methodologies vary across countries and regions, but the overarching goal of secondary education is to prepare students for higher education or vocational training.

In many capital cities, the curriculum for secondary education is designed to be comprehensive and challenging, with a strong emphasis on academic subjects such as mathematics, science, literature, and social studies. Students are often required to take a wide range of courses to help them develop a broad base of knowledge and skills. At the same time, students are also encouraged to pursue their interests through elective courses and extracurricular activities.

Teaching methodologies in secondary education also vary across capital cities, but there has been a growing emphasis on student-centered and project-based learning. This approach encourages students to take an active role in their education, working collaboratively with their peers and teachers to solve real-world problems. This approach has been shown to improve student engagement, critical thinking skills, and problem-solving abilities.

One significant challenge in secondary education is ensuring that students are adequately prepared for the next phase of their education or career. In many capital cities, there is a significant achievement gap between students from different socioeconomic backgrounds, which can impact their chances of success in higher education or the job market. Additionally, preparing students for the demands of the rapidly changing job market is a significant challenge for educators, as technology and automation continue to transform the labor market.

Despite these challenges, there are also many opportunities in secondary education. Many capital cities have implemented innovative programs and initiatives to improve student outcomes and increase equity in education. These include specialized programs for gifted and talented students, career and technical education pathways, and programs designed to support students from disadvantaged backgrounds. By focusing on the unique needs of their students and communities, educators in capital cities are working to provide quality education to all students, regardless of their background or circumstance.

Challenges and opportunities in secondary education

Secondary education is a crucial stage in a student's life as it helps them prepare for higher education and their future careers. However, there are several challenges faced by secondary education systems in capital cities that need to be addressed to ensure the best outcomes for students.

One of the primary challenges faced by secondary education systems in capital cities is the lack of funding and resources. This can result in inadequate facilities, insufficient teaching materials, and limited access to technology, all of which can negatively impact the quality of education offered. Additionally, high student-teacher ratios can make it difficult for teachers to provide personalized attention to each student.

Another challenge is the issue of standardized testing, which has become increasingly prevalent in many capital city education systems. While testing can provide valuable information about student progress, it can also lead to a narrow focus on test preparation rather than a well-rounded education that includes critical thinking, problem-solving, and creativity. Moreover, standardized tests can put undue pressure on students, leading to stress and anxiety.

Despite these challenges, there are also opportunities to improve secondary education in capital cities. One such opportunity is the use of technology to enhance learning. Digital tools, such as online resources and educational apps, can help students access information and learn at their own pace. Moreover, technology can be used to facilitate communication between students and teachers, allowing for more personalized instruction.

Another opportunity is the implementation of innovative teaching methods that can engage students and foster their creativity. For instance, project-based learning and inquiry-based learning can encourage students to think critically and work collaboratively. Furthermore, partnerships between schools and local businesses can provide students with real-world learning experiences and help them develop practical skills.

To address the challenges and seize these opportunities, secondary education systems in capital cities must be willing to adapt and evolve. This may involve restructuring the curriculum, providing more funding and resources, and investing in teacher training and professional development. By doing so, they can ensure that students are well-prepared for higher education and the workforce.

Success stories of secondary schools in the cities

Success stories of secondary schools in capital cities serve as examples of effective educational practices that contribute to students' success. In this chapter, we will highlight some of the best secondary schools in various capital cities and explore the factors that contribute to their success.

One such school is the Harrow School in London, which has a long-standing tradition of academic excellence and producing successful leaders. Their curriculum is based on a broad range of subjects that encourage creativity and critical thinking, and students are also given ample opportunities to develop their leadership and interpersonal skills through extracurricular activities.

Another example is the Lycée Louis-le-Grand in Paris, which has been ranked as the top secondary school in France. The school places a strong emphasis on academic rigor and offers a wide range of advanced courses in various disciplines. The school has also been praised for its inclusive environment, where students from diverse backgrounds are welcomed and supported.

In Tokyo, Japan, the Metropolitan Kokusai High School has gained recognition for its innovative approach to education, which integrates technology and hands-on learning. The school also offers various international programs, allowing students to develop a global perspective and cross-cultural communication skills.

In addition to these examples, we will also explore other success stories of secondary schools in capital cities worldwide and analyze the common factors that contribute to their achievements. By understanding these factors, we can gain valuable insights into how we can improve secondary education in our own communities.

Chapter 3: Higher Education

Overview of higher education system in capital cities

Higher education plays a vital role in the socio-economic development of a country. It enables individuals to acquire advanced skills and knowledge that are essential for the growth of various industries and sectors. In capital cities, the higher education system is generally more developed and diverse compared to other cities, as they attract a larger pool of students and resources. In this chapter, we will provide an overview of the higher education system in capital cities.

Universities and Colleges

Capital cities often have a wide range of universities and colleges that offer various undergraduate and graduate degree programs. These institutions are both public and private, with the former being funded by the government and the latter being funded through tuition fees, donations, and grants. Public universities in capital cities are often among the most prestigious institutions in the country, with a strong focus on research and academic excellence.

Academic Programs

Higher education institutions in capital cities offer a diverse range of academic programs in various fields, including humanities, social sciences, natural sciences, engineering, medicine, law, and business. The academic programs offered are generally of high quality, and students have access to modern facilities and resources such as libraries, laboratories, and research centers. Many universities in capital cities also offer international exchange programs that enable students to study abroad and gain exposure to different cultures and academic systems.

Admission Requirements

Admission requirements for higher education institutions in capital cities vary depending on the institution and program. Generally, admission is highly competitive, and applicants must have a strong academic record, as well as demonstrate extracurricular activities, leadership skills, and community involvement. For international students, additional requirements such as English proficiency tests and visas may be required.

Funding

Funding for higher education institutions in capital cities varies depending on the country and institution. Public universities in capital cities are usually funded by the government, while private universities rely on tuition fees, donations, and grants. Scholarships and financial aid are also available for students who require assistance with tuition fees.

Research and Innovation

Higher education institutions in capital cities are often centers of research and innovation, with a strong focus on developing new knowledge and technologies. They often have partnerships with industry and government agencies to develop and commercialize research findings. The research conducted in these institutions has a significant impact on the local and national economy, as well as on social and cultural development.

In conclusion, the higher education system in capital cities plays a crucial role in shaping the future of a country by producing skilled and knowledgeable graduates who contribute to the growth of various industries and sectors. With a diverse range of institutions, academic programs, and research opportunities, students in capital cities have access to high-quality education and resources that prepare them for successful careers and meaningful contributions to society.

Types of higher education institutions

Higher education institutions in capital cities can take various forms, ranging from traditional universities to specialized colleges and vocational schools. Each type of institution has its own unique strengths and weaknesses, and offers different opportunities for students to pursue their academic and professional goals.

1. Universities

Universities are the most traditional type of higher education institution, and they offer a wide range of academic programs and research opportunities. These institutions typically grant degrees at the undergraduate, graduate, and doctoral levels, and they emphasize academic research and scholarship.

Many capital cities are home to world-renowned universities, such as the University of Tokyo in Japan, the University of Paris in France, and the University of California, Berkeley in the United States. These universities are often major drivers of innovation and economic development in their respective regions, and they attract top talent from around the world.

2. Colleges

Colleges are smaller and more specialized than universities, and they typically focus on undergraduate education. These institutions offer a more personalized academic experience than universities, with smaller class sizes and more opportunities for hands-on learning.

In some cases, colleges may be affiliated with universities and offer courses that can be transferred to a university degree program. In other cases, colleges may offer vocational training in fields such as nursing, engineering, or business.

3. Vocational Schools

Vocational schools are specialized institutions that focus on providing students with practical skills and training for specific careers. These institutions may offer certificate or diploma programs, as well as apprenticeships and on-the-job training.

Vocational schools are particularly important for students who are interested in skilled trades and technical careers, such as plumbing, electrician work, or automotive repair. These schools may also offer training in healthcare fields, such as nursing or medical assisting.

4. Graduate Schools

Graduate schools are institutions that offer advanced academic and professional training beyond the bachelor's degree level. These institutions may offer master's or doctoral degree programs, as well as specialized professional degrees in fields such as law, medicine, or business.

Graduate schools are particularly important for students who are interested in pursuing careers in academia or in specialized professional fields. They offer rigorous academic training and research opportunities, as well as networking opportunities with industry professionals and other experts in the field.

5. Online and Distance Learning Institutions

Online and distance learning institutions are a relatively new type of higher education institution, and they offer flexible and convenient alternatives to traditional classroom-based instruction. These institutions use technology to deliver course content and facilitate communication between students and instructors.

Online and distance learning institutions are particularly important for students who have other commitments, such as work or family obligations, that make traditional classroom-based instruction difficult. They offer a wide range of academic programs, from undergraduate degrees to professional certifications, and they can be accessed from anywhere in the world.

In conclusion, the types of higher education institutions available in capital cities are diverse and offer students a range of opportunities to pursue their academic and professional goals. From traditional universities to specialized colleges and vocational schools, each institution has its own unique strengths and can provide students with valuable knowledge, skills, and experiences.

Popular courses and programs

Higher education institutions in capital cities offer a diverse range of courses and programs that cater to the demands of the local and global job market. Some of the most popular courses and programs offered by universities and colleges in these cities are:

1. Business and Management: Courses in business and management are popular among students who aspire to pursue careers in the corporate world. These courses cover a range of subjects such as accounting, finance, marketing, human resources, and entrepreneurship.

2. Engineering and Technology: With the growing demand for skilled engineers and technologists in various industries, courses in engineering and technology are highly sought after. These courses cover subjects such as mechanical engineering, electrical engineering, computer science, and information technology.

3. Medicine and Health Sciences: Medicine and health sciences are among the most popular fields of study in capital cities. Students can choose from a range of programs such as medicine, nursing, pharmacy, dentistry, and public health.

4. Law: Law is a popular choice for students who want to pursue careers in the legal profession. Courses in law cover a range of subjects such as criminal law, civil law, international law, and human rights.

5. Arts and Humanities: Courses in arts and humanities are popular among students who have a passion for literature, history, philosophy, and the arts. These courses offer students an opportunity to develop critical thinking and analytical skills.

6. Education: Education is a popular field of study for students who aspire to become teachers, educators, and administrators in the education sector. Courses in education cover subjects such as pedagogy, curriculum development, and educational psychology.

7. Environmental Science: With growing concerns about climate change and environmental sustainability, courses in environmental science are gaining popularity. These courses cover a range of subjects such as environmental management, conservation biology, and sustainable development.

These courses and programs are offered by a range of higher education institutions, including universities, colleges, and vocational schools. The choice of institution and program depends on the individual's career goals, interests, and academic background.

Challenges and opportunities in higher education

Higher education plays a vital role in the development of individuals, society, and the economy. However, it also faces several challenges and opportunities in capital cities. One of the main challenges is the increasing cost of higher education, which can limit access to education for individuals from lower socioeconomic backgrounds. This challenge is particularly acute in capital cities, where the cost of living is often high.

Another challenge is the need to keep pace with rapidly changing technology and industries. Higher education institutions must adapt their curricula and teaching methods to prepare students for the demands of the future workforce. This requires significant investment in research and development and collaboration with industry partners.

In addition, internationalization has become a significant opportunity for higher education institutions. With the rise of globalization, students are increasingly seeking international exposure and experience, and universities are looking to attract a diverse student body. Capital cities often have a competitive advantage in this regard, as they are centers of culture, innovation, and opportunity. By attracting international students, institutions can enhance their diversity and international profile, leading to increased funding, research opportunities, and partnerships.

Moreover, the rapid expansion of online learning and the increasing availability of Massive Open Online Courses

(MOOCs) provide new opportunities for higher education institutions. Institutions can use online platforms to reach a broader audience and provide access to education for individuals who might not have been able to attend a traditional campus-based program. However, this shift to online learning also poses challenges, such as ensuring the quality of online courses and maintaining academic integrity.

In conclusion, higher education in capital cities faces both challenges and opportunities. It must adapt to changing technology and industries while also addressing the increasing cost of education and providing access to a diverse student body. By embracing internationalization and leveraging the benefits of online learning, higher education institutions can continue to play a critical role in the development of individuals, society, and the economy.

Success stories of universities and colleges in the cities

Introduction: Chapter 3 of this book focuses on higher education in capital cities around the world. Higher education plays a vital role in shaping the future of a country and its citizens. It is the foundation for producing skilled professionals, researchers, and leaders. In this chapter, we will discuss the overview of higher education systems in capital cities, the types of institutions, popular courses and programs, challenges and opportunities, and success stories of universities and colleges in the cities.

Overview of Higher Education Systems in Capital Cities: Higher education in capital cities is an integral part of their economic, social, and cultural growth. The higher education system in these cities varies depending on the country and its political, social, and economic conditions. Generally, higher education systems in capital cities offer undergraduate and postgraduate degree programs in various disciplines such as science, technology, engineering, mathematics, arts, humanities, social sciences, and business.

Types of Institutions: Higher education institutions in capital cities can be classified into several types, including universities, colleges, technical institutes, and vocational schools. Universities are the highest level of academic institutions that offer undergraduate and postgraduate programs in various fields of study. Colleges, on the other hand, primarily focus on undergraduate education and offer diplomas, certificates, and associate degrees. Technical institutes and vocational schools, on the other hand, offer specialized training in technical and vocational fields.

Popular Courses and Programs: The most popular courses and programs in higher education institutions in capital cities vary depending on the country and its economic conditions. However, some common areas of study that are popular among students worldwide include business administration, engineering, computer science, medicine, law, social sciences, and humanities. In recent years, there has been a growing interest in interdisciplinary programs that combine multiple fields of study, such as environmental studies, global studies, and sustainability studies.

Challenges and Opportunities: Higher education in capital cities faces several challenges, including funding, access, quality, and relevance. Many institutions struggle with funding, as governments often prioritize other sectors such as defense and healthcare. Access to higher education remains a challenge for many students, particularly those from low-income families or marginalized communities. Quality and relevance are also concerns, as some institutions struggle to keep up with changing trends and demands in the job market.

However, there are also opportunities for higher education in capital cities. The growth of technology and digital platforms has created new avenues for learning, such as online education and Massive Open Online Courses (MOOCs).

Governments and institutions are also increasingly prioritizing internationalization, promoting collaborations and partnerships with institutions in other countries.

Success Stories of Universities and Colleges in the Cities: Many universities and colleges in capital cities have achieved significant success in various areas. For example, the University of Tokyo in Japan is known for its excellence in research, particularly in the field of science and technology. The National University of Singapore has consistently been ranked among the top universities in Asia for its innovative teaching and research methods. The University of Oxford in the UK is one of the oldest and most prestigious universities in the world, known for its rigorous academic standards and contributions to various fields of study.

Conclusion: Higher education in capital cities plays a critical role in shaping the future of individuals and societies. It offers opportunities for personal growth, career advancement, and social mobility. However, it also faces several challenges, including funding, access, quality, and relevance. Governments and institutions must work together to address these challenges and create a more inclusive and equitable higher education system that benefits all individuals and communities.

Chapter 4: Research and Innovation

Overview of research and innovation culture in capital cities

Research and innovation are key drivers of economic growth and development, and capital cities play a vital role in fostering a culture of research and innovation. Capital cities around the world are home to some of the most prestigious universities, research centers, and innovation hubs that attract talent and investment from around the globe. These institutions serve as catalysts for technological advancements, new product development, and the creation of new industries.

In the context of research and innovation, capital cities have a number of advantages over other cities. For one, they tend to have higher concentrations of talent, both in terms of researchers and entrepreneurs. This is partly due to the presence of world-class universities and research institutions, which serve as magnets for top talent. In addition, capital cities are often centers of government and industry, which can create opportunities for collaborations and partnerships between researchers and industry experts.

Another advantage of capital cities is the access to funding and resources. Many national governments invest heavily in research and development, and capital cities often receive a larger share of these funds. In addition, capital cities tend to have a greater concentration of venture capital firms and angel investors, which can provide funding for early-stage startups and research projects.

However, capital cities also face a number of challenges when it comes to fostering a culture of research and innovation. One of the biggest challenges is the high cost of living and doing business. This can make it difficult for startups and researchers to find affordable space to work, and can limit the amount of funding available for research and development.

Another challenge is the competition for talent and resources. With so many world-class universities, research institutions, and innovation hubs, capital cities can be very competitive when it comes to attracting and retaining top talent. This can create a "brain drain" effect, where talented individuals move to other cities or countries to pursue better opportunities.

Despite these challenges, capital cities around the world have been successful in fostering a culture of research and innovation. They have done this through a combination of government policies, private sector initiatives, and collaboration between universities, research institutions, and industry experts.

Some examples of successful research and innovation initiatives in capital cities include:

- The Cambridge Science Park in Cambridge, UK, which is home to over 100 companies and research institutions focused on science and technology. The Science Park is a joint venture between the University of Cambridge and Trinity College, and has been instrumental in the growth of the local biotech and IT industries.

- The Massachusetts Institute of Technology (MIT) in Boston, USA, which has a long history of research and innovation in fields such as computer science, engineering, and biotechnology. MIT has spun off over 30,000 companies since its inception, including well-known startups such as Dropbox and 3D printing company Formlabs.

- The Tsukuba Science City in Ibaraki Prefecture, Japan, which was established in 1963 as a planned science and technology city. Today, it is home to over 300 research institutions and companies, and is a hub for research and innovation in fields such as electronics, biotechnology, and energy.

In conclusion, capital cities play a crucial role in fostering a culture of research and innovation. They offer a number of advantages, including access to talent and resources, and can serve as catalysts for technological advancements and new product development. However, they also face a number of challenges, including high costs of living and doing business, and competition for talent and resources. Despite these challenges, capital cities have been successful in promoting research and innovation, and have produced some of the most groundbreaking and innovative discoveries of our time.

Major research institutions and centers

Research and innovation play a crucial role in the development of capital cities. The presence of world-class research institutions and centers attracts top talent and contributes to economic growth and innovation. Here, we will provide an overview of some of the major research institutions and centers in capital cities.

1. National Institutes of Health (NIH), Washington D.C.: The NIH is the largest biomedical research agency in the world, with over 27 institutes and centers conducting research in various areas of health and medicine. The NIH has played a significant role in many breakthroughs, including the discovery of the polio vaccine, the identification of the genetic basis of various diseases, and the development of new cancer therapies.

2. National Science Foundation (NSF), Washington D.C.: The NSF is an independent federal agency that supports research and education across all fields of science and engineering. The agency funds basic research at universities and colleges across the country and provides research grants to scientists and engineers.

3. Massachusetts Institute of Technology (MIT), Boston: MIT is a world-renowned research university known for its cutting-edge research in science, engineering, and technology. The university has produced 95 Nobel laureates and many of its alumni have gone on to found successful companies and startups.

4. University of California, San Francisco (UCSF): UCSF is a leading biomedical research institution, conducting research in various areas of health and medicine. The university has made significant contributions to cancer research, genetics, and neuroscience.

5. Centre National de la Recherche Scientifique (CNRS), Paris: The CNRS is a government-funded research organization that conducts research in all fields of science and technology. The organization is the largest research institution in France and has contributed significantly to research in various areas, including physics, chemistry, biology, and humanities.

6. Max Planck Society, Berlin: The Max Planck Society is a research organization that operates 84 institutes across Germany, conducting research in various areas of science and technology. The organization has made significant contributions to research in physics, chemistry, and neuroscience.

7. Imperial College London, London: Imperial College London is a leading research institution in the United Kingdom, conducting research in various areas of science, engineering, and medicine. The university has made significant contributions to research in areas such as climate change, artificial intelligence, and health.

These are just a few examples of the major research institutions and centers in capital cities. Their presence plays a crucial role in driving innovation and economic growth, attracting top talent, and contributing to the development of capital cities.

Research funding and collaborations

Research funding and collaborations play a crucial role in driving research and innovation in capital cities. The availability of funding and the ease of collaboration with other institutions and organizations can significantly impact the quality and quantity of research being conducted.

One of the primary sources of research funding comes from the government. Governments often allocate funds to research institutions and universities to support research in various fields. The funding may come in the form of grants or contracts, and it is usually based on the merit of the proposed research. In some cases, governments may also collaborate with private organizations to fund research projects.

Another significant source of research funding comes from private organizations, such as corporations and foundations. These organizations may provide grants, sponsor research projects, or even establish their own research centers to support research in a particular field. Private funding often comes with specific objectives and requirements, such as conducting research that aligns with the organization's interests or supporting research that has practical applications.

Collaborations between research institutions and other organizations can also provide opportunities for research funding. For example, collaborations with industry partners may provide funding for research projects that have commercial applications. Collaborations with other universities or research institutions can also lead to joint research projects and funding opportunities.

In addition to funding, collaborations can also provide access to specialized knowledge and resources. Collaborating with other institutions can allow researchers to access specialized equipment, data, or expertise that may not be available at their own institution. Collaborations with industry partners can also provide researchers with access to real-world applications and feedback, which can help to guide their research and make it more relevant to the needs of society.

However, there are also challenges associated with research funding and collaborations. Competition for funding can be intense, and securing funding for research projects can be time-consuming and difficult. Collaborations may also require significant resources, such as time and money, to establish and maintain. In addition, collaborations with industry partners can lead to conflicts of interest, as the research may be influenced by the interests of the industry partner.

Despite these challenges, research funding and collaborations are essential for driving research and innovation in capital cities. By providing access to funding, knowledge, and resources, these collaborations can support groundbreaking research and help to address some of society's most pressing challenges.

Technological innovation and startups in the cities

Technological innovation and startups have become a significant part of the economy in many capital cities. With the rise of technology, there has been a surge in the number of startups in the cities, resulting in a growing focus on technological innovation. Many universities in the capital cities have also played a crucial role in fostering innovation through research, incubation centers, and entrepreneurship programs.

The capital cities have provided an ideal environment for startups, with a vibrant startup culture, access to funding, and a vast pool of talented professionals. Many successful startups have emerged from the capital cities in recent years, such as Uber, Airbnb, and SpaceX. These startups have disrupted their respective industries and transformed the way people live and work.

The availability of funding is a crucial factor in the success of startups. Capital cities have a significant advantage in this regard, as they have access to various funding sources, including venture capital firms, angel investors, and government funding. Moreover, capital cities have a more robust network of support systems for startups, such as accelerators, incubators, and co-working spaces.

Many universities in the capital cities have also established entrepreneurship programs to support and encourage startups. These programs provide students with the resources and tools needed to develop their entrepreneurial skills and launch their startups. Additionally, many universities have established incubation centers to provide startups with physical space and access to resources such as funding, mentoring, and networking opportunities.

The capital cities have also been at the forefront of technological innovation, with a significant number of research institutions and technology centers focusing on cutting-edge research in fields such as artificial intelligence, robotics, and biotechnology. The availability of such resources has enabled startups to leverage the latest technology and stay ahead of the competition.

In conclusion, capital cities have provided a conducive environment for startups and technological innovation. With access to funding, a supportive network of resources, and a vibrant startup culture, capital cities have become the breeding ground for many successful startups that have transformed their respective industries.

Chapter 5: Study Abroad

Overview of study abroad opportunities in capital cities

Studying abroad is an excellent opportunity for students to gain international exposure, develop language skills, and experience a new culture. Capital cities around the world offer various study abroad opportunities for students, ranging from short-term programs to full degree courses. This chapter will provide an overview of study abroad opportunities available in capital cities, including the benefits of studying abroad, the different types of study abroad programs, and the popular destinations for students.

Benefits of studying abroad

Studying abroad offers numerous benefits to students, both academically and personally. Some of the benefits of studying abroad include:

1. Exposure to different cultures: Studying abroad allows students to experience different cultures and ways of life, which broadens their understanding of the world.

2. Language skills: Studying abroad provides students with the opportunity to learn a new language or improve their language skills, which is a valuable asset in today's globalized world.

3. Academic advancement: Studying abroad provides students with the opportunity to take courses that may not be

available in their home country, which can help them to advance their academic and professional goals.

4. Personal growth: Studying abroad challenges students to step out of their comfort zone and develop independence, self-confidence, and adaptability.

Types of study abroad programs

There are various types of study abroad programs available in capital cities, including:

1. Exchange programs: Exchange programs allow students to study at a partner university for a semester or a year. These programs are often reciprocal, meaning that students from the partner university can also study at the home university.

2. Study abroad programs: Study abroad programs are organized by universities or third-party providers and offer students the opportunity to study at a foreign university for a semester, a year, or a summer program.

3. Internship programs: Internship programs allow students to gain practical experience in their field of study while also experiencing a new culture. These programs are often organized by universities or third-party providers.

4. Service-learning programs: Service-learning programs combine academic study with volunteer work in the local community. These programs allow students to contribute to the local community while also gaining academic credit.

Popular destinations for study abroad

Capital cities around the world offer a wide range of study abroad opportunities for students. Some of the popular destinations for study abroad include:

1. London, United Kingdom: London is a popular destination for study abroad due to its diverse culture, world-renowned universities, and opportunities for internships and cultural experiences.

2. Paris, France: Paris is known for its rich history, art, and architecture, making it a popular destination for students interested in the humanities.

3. Tokyo, Japan: Tokyo is a hub of technology and innovation, making it a popular destination for students interested in engineering, computer science, and business.

4. Washington D.C., United States: Washington D.C. is home to numerous international organizations and government agencies, making it a popular destination for students interested in international relations and political science.

Conclusion

Studying abroad provides students with a unique opportunity to gain international exposure, develop language skills, and experience a new culture. Capital cities around the world offer a wide range of study abroad opportunities for students, including exchange programs, study abroad programs, internship programs, and service-learning programs. Popular destinations for study abroad include London, Paris, Tokyo, and Washington D.C. Students who take advantage of study abroad opportunities are likely to gain academic and personal growth, and will have a valuable experience that they will remember for a lifetime.

Popular destinations for international students

Introduction: Studying abroad has become a popular option for students all over the world, and capital cities often offer a wide range of options for international students seeking higher education. This chapter will explore some of the most popular destinations for international students in capital cities, including factors such as quality of education, cost of living, and cultural experiences.

1. London, United Kingdom London is a top destination for international students, with over 100,000 international students studying in the city each year. The city boasts some of the world's most prestigious universities, including University College London, the University of Oxford, and the University of Cambridge. The quality of education in London is exceptional, with a strong focus on research and innovation. Additionally, the city offers a wealth of cultural experiences for students, from visiting world-class museums and art galleries to exploring the city's famous landmarks.

2. Paris, France Paris is another popular destination for international students, with a reputation for excellence in fields such as fashion, design, and art. The city is home to some of the world's most renowned art schools, including École des Beaux-Arts and Parsons Paris. Paris is also known for its vibrant culture, from its world-famous cuisine to its rich history and architecture.

3. Tokyo, Japan Tokyo is a dynamic city with a fast-paced and innovative culture, making it a top destination for students interested in technology, engineering, and business. The city is home to some of the best universities in Asia, including the University of Tokyo and Waseda University. The cost of living in Tokyo can be high, but the city offers a unique cultural experience and a chance to study in a truly international environment.

4. New York City, United States New York City is a hub for international students seeking a diverse and dynamic educational experience. The city is home to some of the world's top universities, including Columbia University, New York University, and The City University of New York. New York City offers a wealth of cultural experiences, from Broadway shows to world-class museums and galleries, and students can take advantage of the city's many internship and networking opportunities.

5. Sydney, Australia Sydney is a popular destination for international students seeking a high-quality education in a beautiful and welcoming city. The city is home to some of the best universities in Australia, including the University of Sydney and the University of New South Wales. Sydney offers a relaxed and friendly atmosphere, with plenty of opportunities for outdoor activities and cultural experiences.

Conclusion: Capital cities around the world offer a diverse range of study abroad opportunities for international students. From London's prestigious universities to Sydney's beautiful beaches, there are countless options for students seeking a unique and enriching educational experience. Factors such as quality of education, cost of living, and cultural experiences all play a role in choosing the right destination, and students should carefully consider their options before making a decision.

Scholarships and financial aid for studying abroad

Studying abroad is an enriching and transformative experience that can broaden horizons, increase cultural competency, and enhance personal and professional development. However, for many students, the cost of studying abroad can be a significant barrier. Fortunately, there are numerous scholarships and financial aid programs available to help make studying abroad more affordable.

In this section, we will explore the various scholarships and financial aid options available for students who wish to study abroad. We will discuss the eligibility requirements, application process, and other important details related to each program.

Types of Scholarships and Financial Aid:

1. Government-funded scholarships: Many countries offer government-funded scholarships for international students. These scholarships may cover tuition fees, living expenses, and travel costs. Some examples of government-funded scholarships include:

- Fulbright Program: The Fulbright Program is one of the most well-known and prestigious scholarship programs in the world. It offers grants to students, scholars, and professionals for the purpose of conducting research, teaching, or studying abroad.

- Chevening Scholarships: The Chevening Scholarships are funded by the UK government and provide full financial support for students to study a one-year master's degree in the UK.

- Erasmus+ Programme: The Erasmus+ Programme is a European Union (EU) funding programme that offers opportunities for students to study or undertake work experience abroad.

1. Institution-specific scholarships: Many universities and colleges have their own scholarship programs for international students. These scholarships may be based on academic merit, financial need, or other criteria. Some examples of institution-specific scholarships include:

- Rhodes Scholarship: The Rhodes Scholarship is a highly competitive scholarship program that offers fully-funded scholarships for postgraduate study at the University of Oxford.

- Gates Cambridge Scholarship: The Gates Cambridge Scholarship is another highly competitive scholarship program that offers fully-funded scholarships for postgraduate study at the University of Cambridge.

- University of Auckland International Student Excellence Scholarship: This scholarship is awarded to international students who have demonstrated academic excellence and who are enrolling in a full-time undergraduate or postgraduate program at the University of Auckland.

1. Private scholarships and grants: There are many private organizations that offer scholarships and grants for international students. These scholarships may be based on a

wide range of criteria, such as academic achievement, community involvement, or specific areas of study. Some examples of private scholarships and grants include:

- The Rotary Foundation Global Grant: The Rotary Foundation Global Grant provides funding for graduate-level academic studies related to one of six areas of focus, including peace and conflict prevention/resolution, disease prevention and treatment, water and sanitation, maternal and child health, basic education and literacy, and economic and community development.

- The Diversity Abroad Network Scholarship: The Diversity Abroad Network Scholarship is awarded to students from diverse backgrounds who are studying abroad.

- The Benjamin A. Gilman International Scholarship: The Benjamin A. Gilman International Scholarship is a need-based scholarship for US citizens who are receiving Pell Grants and who wish to study abroad.

1. Work and study programs: Work and study programs allow students to work while they study, which can help offset the cost of living expenses. Some examples of work and study programs include:

- Working Holiday Visa: The Working Holiday Visa allows students to work and travel in certain countries for a set period of time.

- Co-op programs: Co-op programs allow students to gain work experience related to their field of study while they complete their degree.

Conclusion:

Studying abroad can be an expensive endeavor, but there are many scholarships and financial aid programs available to help make it more affordable. Students should research the various options available to them and apply for as many scholarships and grants as possible to maximize their chances of receiving funding. With the right financial support, studying abroad can be a life-changing experience that opens up new opportunities and possibilities for personal and professional growth.

Cultural experiences and benefits of studying in the cities

Studying abroad has become an increasingly popular option for students seeking a high-quality education and unique cultural experiences. Capital cities around the world offer a range of opportunities for international students, including exposure to diverse cultures, access to renowned universities, and potential career opportunities. In this section, we will explore the cultural experiences and benefits of studying in capital cities.

Cultural Experiences:

One of the primary benefits of studying in a capital city is the opportunity to immerse oneself in a vibrant and diverse cultural environment. Capital cities tend to be cultural and economic hubs, attracting people from all walks of life. As a result, students studying in these cities can experience a variety of cultural events and traditions, from music and art festivals to religious celebrations and cultural parades. For instance, students studying in Paris can visit world-renowned museums and art galleries, attend fashion shows, and enjoy the city's iconic cuisine. In Tokyo, students can experience Japanese cultural festivals, such as cherry blossom viewing, visit historic temples and shrines, and explore the city's vibrant nightlife.

In addition to these cultural experiences, studying in a capital city can also provide students with the opportunity to learn about and appreciate the cultural diversity of their peers.

With students from all over the world, capital cities provide a unique platform for cultural exchange and learning. By interacting with students from different backgrounds and cultures, students can gain a better understanding of different perspectives, worldviews, and ways of life. This can broaden their horizons, help them develop cross-cultural communication skills, and prepare them for a globalized world.

Academic Benefits:

Studying in a capital city can also provide academic benefits to students. Capital cities tend to be home to some of the most renowned universities and research institutions in the world. For example, London has some of the top-ranked universities in the world, including the University of Oxford and University College London. The city is also home to research institutions such as the British Library, which provides students with access to one of the world's largest collections of books and manuscripts. Similarly, Washington D.C. is home to some of the most prestigious universities in the US, including Georgetown University and George Washington University, as well as the Smithsonian Institution, which provides students with access to extensive collections of scientific, historical, and cultural artifacts.

Studying in a capital city can also provide students with opportunities for internships, networking, and potential career opportunities. As capital cities tend to be economic hubs, they are often home to major corporations, government agencies, and international organizations. By studying in a capital city, students can gain access to these organizations, participate in internships, and build professional networks that can lead to future career opportunities.

Challenges and Benefits:

While studying in a capital city can offer a range of cultural and academic benefits, it can also present unique challenges. For instance, students may face higher living costs in these cities, which can be a significant financial burden for many. Additionally, capital cities tend to be more crowded and hectic than other cities, which can be overwhelming for some students. However, these challenges can also provide opportunities for personal growth and development. By learning to navigate a busy and diverse city, students can develop independence, adaptability, and resilience.

Conclusion:

Studying in a capital city can offer a range of cultural, academic, and personal benefits to students. From exposure to diverse cultures to access to world-renowned universities and potential career opportunities, studying in a capital city can provide a unique and enriching experience. However, it is important to consider the challenges and potential drawbacks before making a decision to study abroad in a capital city.

Chapter 6: Vocational and Technical Education
Overview of vocational and technical education system in capital cities

In today's fast-paced world, obtaining a college degree is no longer the only way to secure a good job. Vocational and technical education has become an increasingly popular option for students seeking to acquire skills and knowledge for a specific career path. Vocational and technical education programs are designed to provide students with practical skills and knowledge in a specific trade or profession. In this chapter, we will explore the vocational and technical education system in capital cities and how it differs from traditional academic education.

What is Vocational and Technical Education?

Vocational and technical education is an educational system that focuses on the practical application of skills and knowledge necessary for a particular occupation or trade. The aim of vocational and technical education is to prepare students to enter the workforce immediately after graduation. Unlike traditional academic education, vocational and technical education places a greater emphasis on hands-on training and work experience.

Vocational and technical education programs are usually shorter than traditional academic programs, typically lasting between six months to two years. They may include apprenticeships, on-the-job training, and classroom instruction. Vocational and technical education programs cover a wide range of fields, including healthcare, hospitality, construction, automotive, and technology.

Vocational and Technical Education in Capital Cities

Vocational and technical education is an integral part of the education system in capital cities. In most capital cities, vocational and technical education is offered through specialized schools, community colleges, and vocational training centers. These institutions provide students with the necessary skills and knowledge to enter the workforce in specific fields.

In some capital cities, vocational and technical education is integrated into high school programs, allowing students to gain practical skills and experience while still in school. This provides students with the opportunity to explore different career paths and gain hands-on experience in a particular field.

Types of Vocational and Technical Programs

Vocational and technical education programs vary depending on the field of study. Some of the most common vocational and technical programs in capital cities include:

1. Healthcare: Programs in healthcare include nursing, medical assisting, dental hygiene, and medical coding and billing.

2. Technology: Programs in technology include computer programming, web design, and cybersecurity.

3. Skilled Trades: Programs in skilled trades include plumbing, electrical work, carpentry, and welding.

4. Hospitality and Tourism: Programs in hospitality and tourism include culinary arts, hospitality management, and travel and tourism.

Job Prospects and Career Opportunities

Vocational and technical education prepares students for careers in specific fields. Graduates of vocational and technical education programs have a higher chance of finding employment than graduates of traditional academic programs. According to the National Center for Education Statistics, the employment rate for students with vocational and technical education is higher than that of students with traditional academic education.

The demand for skilled workers in various industries is on the rise, making vocational and technical education a viable option for students seeking a successful career path. Graduates of vocational and technical education programs can find employment in various fields, including healthcare, technology, skilled trades, and hospitality.

Conclusion

The vocational and technical education system in capital cities provides students with practical skills and knowledge necessary to enter the workforce immediately after graduation. Vocational and technical education programs are designed to prepare students for specific careers, and graduates have a higher chance of finding employment than graduates of traditional academic programs. With the growing demand for skilled workers in various industries, vocational and technical education is a viable option for students seeking a successful career path.

Types of vocational and technical programs

Introduction Vocational and technical education programs provide students with specialized skills and knowledge in specific fields that prepare them for a career path. In this chapter, we will provide an overview of the types of vocational and technical programs available in capital cities.

Apprenticeship Programs Apprenticeship programs are one of the oldest forms of vocational education. Apprenticeships provide a combination of on-the-job training and classroom instruction. Apprenticeships are available in a variety of trades, such as construction, plumbing, electrical work, and automotive repair. Apprenticeships are usually three to five years in duration, and apprentices are paid a wage while they are working.

Community College Programs Community colleges offer a range of vocational and technical programs that can lead to an associate degree or certification. Community colleges offer programs in fields such as healthcare, business, information technology, and transportation. Community college programs are generally shorter in duration than four-year college programs and are more affordable.

Career and Technical Education (CTE) Programs CTE programs are designed to prepare students for specific career paths. CTE programs are available in high schools and post-secondary institutions. These programs offer training in fields such as healthcare, business, construction, and automotive repair. CTE programs usually include a combination of classroom instruction and hands-on training.

Continuing Education Programs Continuing education programs are designed for individuals who are already working in a specific field and want to update their skills or learn new ones. These programs are available through community colleges, trade schools, and professional organizations. Continuing education programs are available in a wide range of fields, such as healthcare, technology, and business.

Trade Schools Trade schools are private institutions that offer vocational education programs in specific fields. Trade schools offer programs in fields such as automotive repair, culinary arts, cosmetology, and HVAC (heating, ventilation, and air conditioning) repair. Trade schools are generally shorter in duration than four-year college programs and are more focused on hands-on training.

Conclusion Vocational and technical education programs provide students with specialized skills and knowledge in specific fields that prepare them for a career path. In capital cities, there are a variety of vocational and technical education programs available, including apprenticeship programs, community college programs, CTE programs, continuing education programs, and trade schools. These programs offer students the opportunity to gain practical, hands-on experience in a variety of fields, preparing them for success in their chosen career.

Job prospects and career opportunities

Vocational and technical education plays a crucial role in preparing students for employment in specific fields. It is designed to provide hands-on training and practical skills to students who wish to pursue careers in various trades, such as construction, automotive repair, nursing, information technology, and many others. In this section, we will explore the job prospects and career opportunities available to graduates of vocational and technical programs in capital cities.

Job Prospects:

One of the biggest advantages of vocational and technical education is that it provides graduates with specific skills that are in high demand in the job market. Many industries require workers with specialized skills, and graduates of vocational and technical programs are often the ideal candidates for these positions. For example, graduates of nursing programs can find employment in hospitals, nursing homes, and other healthcare facilities. Graduates of automotive repair programs can work in auto repair shops or as technicians in dealerships. Graduates of information technology programs can work in a variety of IT-related fields, including software development, cybersecurity, and network administration.

The job prospects for graduates of vocational and technical programs vary depending on the specific field of study. However, in general, there is a high demand for skilled workers in many industries, and this demand is expected to continue to grow in the coming years. According to the Bureau of Labor Statistics (BLS), employment in many vocational and technical fields is projected to grow faster than the average for all occupations.

Career Opportunities:

Graduates of vocational and technical programs can pursue a variety of career paths, depending on their interests and skills. Some graduates may choose to work in their chosen field immediately after graduation, while others may choose to further their education by pursuing a bachelor's or master's degree.

In addition to traditional job opportunities, vocational and technical education can also provide graduates with the skills and knowledge to start their own businesses. For example, graduates of culinary arts programs can start their own restaurants or catering businesses, while graduates of construction programs can start their own contracting companies.

Another advantage of vocational and technical education is that it can lead to high-paying jobs. Many skilled trades are in high demand, and employers are willing to pay top dollar for workers with the right skills and experience. For example, according to the BLS, the median annual wage for electricians was $56,900 in May 2020, while the median annual wage for HVAC technicians was $50,590.

Conclusion:

Vocational and technical education offers a range of job prospects and career opportunities for graduates. It provides hands-on training and practical skills that are in high demand in many industries. Graduates of vocational and technical programs can pursue careers in a variety of fields, start their own businesses, or further their education by pursuing a bachelor's or master's degree. In addition, vocational and technical education can lead to high-paying jobs, making it an attractive option for those looking to enter the workforce.

Challenges and opportunities in vocational and technical education

Vocational and technical education (VTE) has become increasingly important in recent years as a means of equipping students with the practical skills needed to succeed in the workforce. However, VTE also faces a number of challenges and opportunities in the capital cities. This section will examine some of the key challenges and opportunities facing VTE in these cities.

Challenges:

1. Perception: One of the major challenges facing VTE is the perception that it is a lesser form of education. Many parents and students still believe that academic education is the only path to success and that vocational education is only for those who are not academically inclined. This perception needs to change, and VTE must be seen as an equally valuable and viable option for students.

2. Funding: Funding for VTE is often inadequate, and this has a direct impact on the quality of education provided. Without sufficient funding, schools are unable to offer the latest technology, equipment, and resources necessary for training students for the modern workforce.

3. Curriculum: Curriculum for VTE programs is often outdated and not aligned with industry standards. To ensure that students are adequately prepared for the workforce, VTE

programs must constantly evolve to meet the changing needs of employers.

4. Quality of teaching: The quality of teaching in VTE programs varies widely. Many teachers lack the necessary skills and experience to teach practical skills effectively. To ensure that students receive quality education, it is important to attract and retain experienced teachers who have industry-specific skills and knowledge.

5. Perception of employers: Employers may perceive VTE graduates as lacking the necessary academic skills to succeed in the workplace. This perception needs to change, and employers must recognize the value of practical skills that VTE graduates possess.

Opportunities:

1. Flexibility: VTE programs are often more flexible than traditional academic programs, allowing students to work part-time or attend classes in the evening. This flexibility allows students to gain practical experience while still pursuing their education.

2. Collaboration with employers: VTE programs offer a unique opportunity for collaboration between educators and employers. By working closely with employers, VTE programs can ensure that students are being trained with the skills necessary for success in the workforce.

3. Technology: Technology has the potential to revolutionize VTE by providing students with access to the

latest tools and resources. Online learning platforms, virtual simulations, and other technological innovations can enhance the learning experience and prepare students for the modern workplace.

4. High demand for skilled workers: The demand for skilled workers in many industries is high, and VTE graduates are well-positioned to fill these positions. By providing students with the practical skills needed to succeed in these industries, VTE programs can help bridge the skills gap and provide valuable employment opportunities.

5. Career pathways: VTE programs can offer clear career pathways for students, providing a roadmap for success in the workforce. By aligning with industry standards and providing opportunities for work-based learning, VTE programs can help students build the skills and experience needed to succeed in their chosen career.

Conclusion:

Despite the challenges facing VTE in the capital cities, there are also significant opportunities for growth and development. By addressing the challenges and capitalizing on the opportunities, VTE programs can provide students with the skills and experience needed to succeed in the modern workforce. To ensure the success of VTE, it is important to shift the perception of vocational education, increase funding, update curriculum, attract quality teachers, and work closely

with employers to provide students with the skills needed to
succeed in the workforce.

Chapter 7: Education Policies and Governance
Overview of education policies and governance in capital cities

Education policies and governance play a crucial role in shaping the education system of a country. Capital cities usually have a different system of education policies and governance as compared to the rest of the country. This is because capital cities serve as the center of power and decision-making, and education policies are often developed and implemented here. In this chapter, we will provide an overview of education policies and governance in capital cities.

Overview of Education Policies:

Education policies refer to the guidelines, principles, and regulations that govern the provision and delivery of education in a country. In capital cities, education policies are developed and implemented by the national government or the local government, depending on the education system in place. For instance, in some countries, the education system is centralized, and the national government is responsible for developing and implementing education policies, while in others, the education system is decentralized, and local governments have more autonomy in developing and implementing education policies.

Education policies in capital cities cover a wide range of areas, including curriculum development, teacher training, assessment and evaluation, financing, and governance. These policies are developed to ensure that the education system meets the needs of learners and the society.

Governance of Education:

Governance of education refers to the system of decision-making and management of education. In capital cities, the governance of education is often centralized, with the national government having more power and authority in making decisions related to education. However, the level of decentralization varies depending on the education system in place.

In some countries, education is managed at the local level, with local governments having more autonomy in making decisions related to education. In such cases, the role of the national government is to provide guidelines and support to ensure that education policies are implemented effectively.

The governance of education in capital cities also involves the participation of various stakeholders, including parents, teachers, students, and the private sector. These stakeholders play an essential role in the decision-making process and the implementation of education policies.

Challenges in Education Policies and Governance:

Despite the efforts made to develop and implement education policies, several challenges remain. Some of these challenges include:

1. Limited Resources: Education policies often require a significant amount of resources to implement effectively.

Limited resources, especially in developing countries, can hinder the implementation of education policies and lead to disparities in the education system.

2. Inadequate Infrastructure: Inadequate infrastructure, such as classrooms, libraries, and laboratories, can also hinder the implementation of education policies. This is especially true in developing countries, where the education system is often underfunded.

3. Inadequate Training: Inadequate training of teachers and other education stakeholders can also hinder the implementation of education policies. Teachers need to be trained regularly to ensure that they have the necessary skills and knowledge to implement education policies effectively.

4. Political Instability: Political instability can also hinder the development and implementation of education policies. In countries where there is political instability, education policies are often given less priority, leading to disparities in the education system.

Opportunities in Education Policies and Governance:

Despite the challenges, there are several opportunities in education policies and governance in capital cities. Some of these opportunities include:

1. Innovative Approaches: Capital cities often have access to more resources and a higher level of expertise. This provides an opportunity to develop and implement innovative approaches to education policies and governance.

2. International Cooperation: International cooperation can also provide an opportunity for capital cities to learn from other countries' experiences and implement best practices.

3. Private Sector Participation: Private sector participation in education policies and governance can also provide an opportunity to increase resources and improve the quality of education.

Conclusion:

Education policies and governance play a crucial role in shaping the education system of a country. In capital cities, education policies are often developed and implemented by the national government or the local government. The policies and governance framework in these cities aim to provide equitable access to education, promote quality education, and prepare students for the workforce. However, there are several challenges that need to be addressed, such as funding constraints, outdated curriculum, and inadequate teacher training. Despite these challenges, capital cities are home to some of the best education systems in the world, with highly reputable universities and research institutions. It is essential for policymakers and educators to continue to work together to address the challenges and leverage the opportunities to ensure that the education system in capital cities continues to thrive.

Continuation:

Education policies and governance in capital cities are often influenced by the national policies and priorities. The national government in most countries sets the overall education policy framework, while the local government is responsible for implementing these policies at the local level. In some cases, the local government may have some autonomy to develop and implement education policies that meet the specific needs of their community. However, this may create a disparity in the quality of education between different regions within the city or country.

Furthermore, education policies and governance in capital cities must address the changing needs of the society and the economy. The current digital revolution and the emergence of new industries require a shift in the education system to provide students with the necessary skills and competencies to thrive in the workforce. There is a need for a stronger focus on science, technology, engineering, and mathematics (STEM) education to meet the growing demand for skilled professionals in these areas. In addition, education policies and governance must also address the increasing demand for lifelong learning and reskilling to keep up with the rapidly changing job market.

Another critical aspect of education policies and governance in capital cities is the need to promote diversity, equity, and inclusion in education. This involves ensuring that education policies and practices do not discriminate against individuals based on their race, gender, socioeconomic status, or other factors. Education policies should aim to promote inclusive education that caters to the diverse needs of students and provides equal opportunities for all. This includes providing access to education for students with disabilities, indigenous students, and students from marginalized communities.

In conclusion, education policies and governance in capital cities must be adaptable to the changing needs of the society and the economy. There is a need for policies that promote STEM education, lifelong learning, and diversity, equity, and inclusion in education. It is essential for policymakers and educators to work together to address the challenges and leverage the opportunities to ensure that the education system in capital cities continues to provide equitable access to quality education and prepares students for the workforce.

Roles and responsibilities of government and non-governmental organizations

Education policies and governance are not only the responsibility of the government, but also involve non-governmental organizations (NGOs) and other stakeholders. In this chapter, we will explore the roles and responsibilities of both the government and NGOs in the development and implementation of education policies in capital cities. We will also examine the benefits and challenges of partnerships between these two entities in the education sector.

Government's role in education policy and governance:

The government's role in education policy and governance is critical. Governments develop and implement policies that regulate the education sector, including curriculum development, teacher training, and quality assurance. Governments also provide funding for education and allocate resources for schools and universities. The role of the government is to ensure that education is accessible, equitable, and of high quality for all students.

In many capital cities, the national government is responsible for education policy and governance. The national government sets the standards and regulations for education and provides funding for education. Local governments, such as city or regional governments, may also have a role in education policy and governance, particularly in areas such as school infrastructure and teacher employment.

NGOs' role in education policy and governance:

NGOs play a vital role in education policy and governance, particularly in advocating for the rights of students and ensuring access to education for all. NGOs can be involved in policy development, implementation, and monitoring, and can provide critical support to the government in areas such as teacher training, curriculum development, and community engagement.

In many capital cities, NGOs are involved in education policy and governance. NGOs can be involved in lobbying the government for policy changes, monitoring the implementation of policies, and providing support to schools and students. NGOs may also provide direct services, such as teacher training, curriculum development, and advocacy for the rights of marginalized students.

Partnerships between government and NGOs:

Partnerships between government and NGOs can be beneficial for the education sector. These partnerships can lead to the development of more effective policies, more efficient use of resources, and improved access to education for all students. Partnerships can also facilitate communication between different stakeholders and ensure that the needs of all students are met.

However, partnerships between government and NGOs can also pose challenges. NGOs may have different priorities and approaches than the government, which can lead to conflicts. Additionally, partnerships may be limited by funding constraints and political instability.

Conclusion:

In conclusion, both the government and NGOs play critical roles in education policy and governance in capital cities. The government is responsible for developing and implementing policies that regulate the education sector, while NGOs provide critical support and advocacy for students. Partnerships between government and NGOs can be beneficial, but also pose challenges. As the education sector continues to evolve, it is essential that the government and NGOs work together to ensure that education is accessible, equitable, and of high quality for all students.

Funding and budget allocation for education

Education is a crucial sector for any country's development, and its importance cannot be overstated. Proper funding and budget allocation play a vital role in providing quality education and ensuring equal access to all students. The funding and budget allocation for education can be divided into two broad categories, namely government funding and private funding. In this chapter, we will discuss the funding and budget allocation for education in the capital cities of various countries.

Government funding:

Government funding is the primary source of funding for education in most countries. The government funding for education includes both direct and indirect funding. Direct funding refers to the money allocated to the education sector in the government's annual budget. Indirect funding includes tax exemptions, subsidies, and grants to educational institutions.

The amount of government funding for education varies from country to country. In some countries, the government spends a significant portion of its budget on education, while in others, education receives a much smaller percentage of the budget. For example, according to the UNESCO Institute for Statistics, in 2018, the United States spent approximately 5.9% of its GDP on education, while in Finland, the percentage was approximately 6.8%.

Private funding:

Apart from government funding, private funding is also a significant source of funding for education in many countries. Private funding for education includes donations from individuals, corporations, and philanthropic organizations. Private funding can also come in the form of tuition fees paid by students attending private educational institutions.

In some countries, private funding for education is more significant than government funding. For example, in the United States, private funding for higher education is a significant source of revenue for many universities and colleges.

Budget allocation:

The budget allocation for education is the process of determining how the funds allocated to the education sector will be spent. The budget allocation for education depends on several factors, including the number of students, the type of education, and the needs of the education system.

In some countries, the budget allocation for education is based on the number of students enrolled in each level of education. In other countries, the budget allocation is based on the needs of the education system. For example, some countries allocate more funds to research and development in the education sector.

Challenges in funding and budget allocation:

Despite the importance of education and the need for adequate funding and budget allocation, many challenges exist in this area. One of the significant challenges is the competition for resources. Education competes with other sectors for funding, and education may not always be a priority for governments.

Another challenge is the lack of transparency in budget allocation. In some countries, it is challenging to determine how much funding has been allocated to the education sector and how it has been spent. This lack of transparency can make it difficult to hold governments accountable for their spending decisions.

Conclusion:

Funding and budget allocation play a critical role in providing quality education and ensuring equal access to education for all students. Government funding is the primary source of funding for education, but private funding is also significant in many countries. The budget allocation for education is determined based on several factors, including the number of students, the type of education, and the needs of the education system. Despite the importance of education and the need for adequate funding and budget allocation, many challenges exist in this area, including competition for resources and lack of transparency.

Evaluation and improvement of educational programs and policies

Introduction: Evaluation and improvement of educational programs and policies is a crucial aspect of education governance. It helps to ensure that the education system is functioning effectively and meeting the needs of students and society. In this chapter, we will explore the importance of evaluation and improvement in education policies and programs in capital cities.

Importance of Evaluation and Improvement: Evaluation and improvement of educational programs and policies are critical for several reasons. Firstly, it helps to ensure that the educational system is achieving its goals and objectives. Evaluation helps to determine whether the policies and programs are effective in improving student outcomes, such as academic achievement, skills development, and employability. Secondly, evaluation provides feedback to policymakers and education practitioners to identify areas for improvement. This helps in making informed decisions on resource allocation, curriculum design, teacher training, and other aspects of education policy and practice. Thirdly, evaluation and improvement promote accountability and transparency in the education system. It allows stakeholders, including parents, students, and employers, to assess the effectiveness of educational policies and programs and hold education authorities accountable for their performance.

Types of Evaluation: There are different types of evaluation that can be used to assess the effectiveness of educational policies and programs. These include:

1. Formative Evaluation: This type of evaluation is conducted during the development and implementation of educational policies and programs. It helps to identify potential problems and challenges that may arise during implementation and provides feedback to policymakers to make necessary adjustments. Formative evaluation is essential to ensure that policies and programs are effective and meet the needs of students.

2. Summative Evaluation: This type of evaluation is conducted at the end of an educational program or policy. It assesses the overall effectiveness of the program or policy in achieving its objectives. Summative evaluation is essential to determine whether the program or policy should be continued, modified, or discontinued.

3. Process Evaluation: This type of evaluation assesses how well the educational program or policy is being implemented. It helps to identify areas of strength and weaknesses in the implementation process and provides feedback to policymakers to make necessary adjustments.

4. Impact Evaluation: This type of evaluation assesses the extent to which the educational program or policy has achieved its intended outcomes. It helps to determine the effectiveness of the program or policy in improving student

outcomes, such as academic achievement, skills development, and employability.

Improvement Strategies: Evaluation is only useful if the findings are acted upon to improve educational policies and programs. Some of the strategies that can be used to improve education policies and programs include:

1. Feedback Mechanisms: Developing feedback mechanisms that allow stakeholders to provide feedback on the effectiveness of educational policies and programs. This helps policymakers to identify areas for improvement and make necessary adjustments.

2. Continuous Improvement: Implementing continuous improvement processes that allow for regular assessments and improvements to educational policies and programs.

3. Capacity Building: Providing capacity building opportunities to education practitioners to improve their skills and knowledge in the design, implementation, and evaluation of educational policies and programs.

4. Research and Development: Investing in research and development to identify innovative approaches to improving educational policies and programs.

Conclusion: Evaluation and improvement of educational policies and programs are essential for ensuring that the education system is effective and meeting the needs of students and society. Capital cities must develop and implement effective evaluation strategies and improvement strategies to ensure that their education systems are effective, efficient, and of high quality. It requires collaboration and partnership among stakeholders, including government, non-governmental organizations, educators, and researchers, to achieve the desired outcomes.

Conclusion
Recap of the educational landscape of capital cities

Throughout this report, we have explored the educational landscape of capital cities across the world, focusing on the various levels of education, including primary, secondary, higher education, vocational and technical education, and study abroad opportunities. We have also examined the role of research and innovation, education policies and governance, and the challenges and opportunities faced by the educational systems of these cities.

Capital cities often represent the most developed and sophisticated education systems of their respective countries, with a greater number of educational institutions, resources, and opportunities. These cities often house some of the world's most prestigious universities, research institutions, and technical colleges, attracting both local and international students.

The primary education systems in capital cities often have higher enrollment rates, with greater access to resources, facilities, and qualified teachers. The secondary education systems, although more competitive, offer a diverse range of educational programs, including vocational and technical programs that prepare students for employment opportunities.

The higher education systems in capital cities offer a broad range of degree programs, with many universities recognized globally for their research output, academic standards, and international collaborations. Moreover, the cities are home to various research institutions and centers, with extensive research funding and collaborations that promote technological innovation, startups, and economic growth.

Studying abroad in capital cities offers students an opportunity to experience different cultures, acquire new perspectives, and gain exposure to diverse educational systems. The cities offer various scholarships and financial aid options, making studying abroad accessible to students from diverse backgrounds.

Education policies and governance play a critical role in shaping the education systems of capital cities. Governments and non-governmental organizations have significant roles and responsibilities in funding, implementing, and evaluating education policies and programs. The evaluation and improvement of educational programs and policies are essential for the continued growth and development of the educational systems of these cities.

In conclusion, the educational landscape of capital cities is diverse and complex, offering various opportunities and challenges. However, with the proper policies and funding, education systems in these cities have the potential to make a significant impact on the economic, social, and cultural development of their respective countries. The educational systems of these cities will continue to play a critical role in shaping the future of the next generation of leaders, innovators, and entrepreneurs.

Key takeaways and lessons learned

Throughout this comprehensive examination of the educational landscape of capital cities, several key takeaways and lessons learned have emerged. Here are some of the most important points to remember:

1. Education is crucial for individual and societal development: Access to quality education is essential for personal growth and development, as well as for the advancement of society as a whole. In capital cities, education systems often play a critical role in shaping national and international policy.

2. Capital cities offer diverse educational opportunities: Capital cities around the world are home to a range of educational institutions, from world-renowned universities to vocational and technical schools, that offer diverse opportunities for learners at all levels.

3. Research and innovation are essential for progress: Capital cities often house major research institutions and centers that are at the forefront of cutting-edge discoveries and technological advancements, making them hotbeds of innovation and creativity.

4. Study abroad is an enriching experience: Studying abroad in capital cities provides students with an immersive cultural experience that can broaden their perspectives and enhance their personal and professional growth.

5. Vocational and technical education is an important career pathway: Vocational and technical education programs offer valuable skills training and job opportunities for students who may not be interested in pursuing traditional academic pathways.

6. Education policies and governance are critical for success: Effective education policies and governance structures are necessary for the efficient and equitable operation of education systems in capital cities and beyond.

In conclusion, the educational landscape of capital cities is complex and multifaceted, offering a diverse array of opportunities for learners at all stages of life. By understanding the unique strengths and challenges of education systems in capital cities, policymakers and educators can work together to create systems that are inclusive, equitable, and effective in meeting the needs of all learners. Ultimately, by investing in education, we invest in the future of our communities, our countries, and our world.

Future outlook for education and academia in the cities

As capital cities continue to grow and develop, the education and academia landscape will also evolve. Here are some potential future trends and developments to keep an eye on:

1. Emphasis on digital learning: With the rise of technology and online learning platforms, the use of digital tools and resources will continue to play a larger role in education. This includes online courses, virtual classrooms, and educational apps.

2. Focus on STEM education: As technology continues to advance and shape our world, there will be an increasing demand for individuals skilled in science, technology, engineering, and math (STEM). Expect to see more programs and initiatives geared towards STEM education.

3. Greater collaboration between academia and industry: To better prepare students for the workforce, there will be a greater emphasis on collaboration between academia and industry. This can include partnerships, internships, and co-op programs.

4. Increase in international student enrollment: As globalization continues to impact the world, there will be a growing demand for international education. Capital cities, with their diverse populations and strong education systems,

will likely continue to attract a large number of international students.

5. Focus on inclusivity and diversity: With growing awareness and attention on issues of diversity and inclusivity, there will likely be a greater emphasis on creating education systems that are accessible and welcoming to all students, regardless of their background or identity.

6. Greater emphasis on vocational and technical education: As the job market continues to evolve, there will be a greater need for individuals skilled in specific trades and technical areas. Vocational and technical education will become increasingly important in preparing students for these careers.

7. Increased attention on mental health and well-being: As awareness of mental health issues continues to grow, there will be a greater emphasis on creating education systems that prioritize student well-being. This can include initiatives focused on mental health support, mindfulness, and wellness education.

In conclusion, the education and academia landscape in capital cities is diverse, dynamic, and constantly evolving. While there are many challenges and opportunities facing these systems, there is also a great deal of potential for growth and innovation. By staying up-to-date on trends and developments, educators and policymakers can work towards creating education systems that are accessible, inclusive, and effective for all students.

THE END

Key Terms and Definitions

To help you better understand the language and concepts related to aging and older adults, below you will find a list of key terms and their definitions.

Key Terms and Definitions:

1. Education landscape: The overall environment of the education system, including the institutions, policies, programs, and stakeholders involved in providing education.

2. Capital cities: The cities that serve as the administrative and political center of a country, usually home to the government, legislature, and other important institutions.

3. Primary education: The first stage of formal education, usually aimed at children aged 5-11, focused on basic literacy and numeracy skills.

4. Secondary education: The second stage of formal education, usually aimed at teenagers aged 11-18, providing more specialized knowledge and skills than primary education.

5. Tertiary education: The third and final stage of formal education, usually provided by universities, colleges, and vocational schools, aimed at providing advanced knowledge and skills for a particular profession or field of study.

6. Vocational education: Education and training that is focused on developing practical skills for a particular occupation or trade, often through hands-on learning experiences.

7. Technical education: Education and training that is focused on developing skills and knowledge in a specific field of technology, such as engineering or computer science.

8. STEM education: Education that is focused on science, technology, engineering, and mathematics, aimed at preparing students for careers in these fields.

9. International education: Education that is provided to students from different countries and cultural backgrounds, often involving language learning and exposure to different cultural perspectives.

10. Research and innovation: The process of developing new knowledge, products, or services through scientific or creative inquiry, often involving collaboration between academic and industry partners.

Supporting Materials

Introduction:

- Organisation for Economic Co-operation and Development (2019). Education at a Glance 2019: OECD Indicators. OECD Publishing.

Chapter 1: Primary Education

- UNESCO (2016). Education for people and planet: Creating sustainable futures for all. Global Education Monitoring Report. Paris, UNESCO.

- National Center for Education Statistics (2019). Digest of Education Statistics, 2018 (NCES 2020-009). U.S. Department of Education.

Chapter 2: Secondary Education

- Organisation for Economic Co-operation and Development (2018). PISA 2018 Results (Volume I): What Students Know and Can Do. OECD Publishing.

- Schleicher, A. (2018). World Class: How to Build a 21st-Century School System. Strong Performers and Successful Reformers in Education. Paris, OECD Publishing.

Chapter 3: Higher Education

- UNESCO (2015). Rethinking Education: Towards a global common good? Global Education Monitoring Report. Paris, UNESCO.

- Altbach, P.G. & Knight, J. (2007). The internationalization of higher education: Motivations and realities. Journal of Studies in International Education, 11(3-4), 290-305.

Chapter 4: Research and Innovation

- World Intellectual Property Organization (2019). World Intellectual Property Report 2019 - The Geography of Innovation: Local Hotspots, Global Networks. Geneva, WIPO.
- European Commission (2018). Innovation performance: Why regions matter. Regional Innovation Scoreboard 2017. Brussels, European Commission.

Chapter 5: Study Abroad

- Institute of International Education (2020). Open Doors 2020: Report on International Educational Exchange. IIE.
- United Nations Educational, Scientific and Cultural Organization (2019). Global Education Monitoring Report 2019: Migration, displacement and education: Building bridges, not walls. Paris, UNESCO.

Chapter 6: Vocational and Technical Education

- Organisation for Economic Co-operation and Development (2019). OECD Reviews of Vocational Education and Training: Mexico 2018. OECD Publishing.
- World Economic Forum (2020). The Future of Jobs Report 2020. Geneva, World Economic Forum.

Chapter 7: Education Policies and Governance

- World Bank (2018). World Development Report 2018: Learning to Realize Education's Promise. Washington, DC, World Bank Group.
- Baker, D.P. & Wiseman, A.W. (2016). Education Governance for the Twenty-First Century: Overcoming the Structural

Barriers to School Reform. Education Policy Analysis Archives, 24(87), 1-25.

Conclusion:

- United Nations Educational, Scientific and Cultural Organization (2020). Futures of Education: Learning to Become. Paris, UNESCO.

- Organisation for Economic Co-operation and Development (2020). Education Policy Outlook 2020: Putting Student Learning at the Centre. OECD Publishing.